Baseball SUPERSTARS 20X15

By K. C. Kelley

SCHOLASTIC

PHOTO CREDITS:

Photos ©: cover background lights and throughout: winui/Shutterstock, Inc.; cover background stadium: Kalawin/ iStockphoto; cover left: Otto Greule Jr/Getty Images; cover center: Chris Szagola/AP Images; cover right: Chris Bernacchi/AP Images; back cover baseballs, 1 center and throughout: Tomislav Forgo/Shutterstock, Inc.; 1 bottom: Kalawin/iStockphoto; 5: Kathy Willens/AP Images; 7: Mike Buscher/Newscom; 9: Jim McIsaac/Getty Images; 11: Mitchell Layton/Getty Images; 13: John Sleezer/Kansas City Star/Newscom; 15: Tom Pennington/Getty Images; 17: Louis Lopez/CALSP/AP Images; 19: John Fisher/CALSP/AP Images; 21: G Fiume/Getty Images; 23: Boston Globe/Getty Images; 25: Ric Tapia/Icon SMI 269/Newscom; 27: Lynne Sladky/AP Images; 29: Chris O'Meara/AP Images; 30 top: Al Bello/Getty Images; 30 bottom: Jim McIsaac/Getty Images; 31 top: Jamie Sabau/Getty Images; 31 bottom: G Fiume/Getty Images.

Designed by Cheung Tai
Photo Editor: Cynthia Carris

Library of Congress Cataloging-in-Publication Data available

ISBN 978-0-545-83898-6

10 9 8 7 6 5 4 3 2 1   15 16 17 18 19

Printed in the U.S.A.   40
First printing, September 2015

TABLE OF CONTENTS

Stats Notes:
Note: All statistics are complete through the 2014 MLB season.
ERA = Earned Run Average
WHIP = Walks + Hits per Inning Pitched
OPS = On-base Percentage plus Slugging average

Madison Bumgarner

PITCHER | SAN FRANCISCO GIANTS

THROWS: LEFT	BATS: RIGHT	
HEIGHT: 6' 5"	WEIGHT: 235 LBS	HOMETOWN: HICKORY, NC

The best players play their best when the pressure is on. They come through in the clutch and do things that even their biggest fans think is impossible. The World Series has never seen such a stretch of big-game pitching like the one Madison Bumgarner performed in 2014. In nine days, he became a legend.

Bumgarner started and won Game 1 for the Giants, allowing only three hits in seven innings. He won Game 5, giving up only four hits while going all nine innings. But the Kansas City Royals forced a deciding Game 7. In the fifth inning, manager Bruce Bochy turned to his ace. Even though he had thrown a complete game just three days before, he stayed on the mound inning after

HISTORY LESSON

The best comparison to Bumgarner's 2014 World Series came way back in 1905. The New York Giants' Christy Mathewson threw three shutouts in six days over the Philadelphia Athletics.

inning. He ended up pitching the final five innings of the game and earning the longest save in World Series history! Bumgarner was the obvious choice as the 2014 World Series MVP. (That followed his MVP trophy from the 2014 NLCS, too!)

Bumgarner also pitched in the 2010 World Series. He is now the best World Series pitcher ever. He capped off a magical 2014 by being named *Sports Illustrated*'s Sportsman of the Year.

Not bad for a kid who grew up on a farm in North Carolina. He still spends his off-season there. In 2006, a Giants scout saw him playing in a high school game. Bumgarner was not the winning pitcher, but he hit two home runs! San Francisco picked him in the first round of the 2007 draft. He joined the big-league rotation for good in 2010 and has at least 13 wins in each season since. He is the best big-game pitcher in baseball today.

BASEBALL CARD!

Made the Majors in . . .	2009
Wins	67
Strikeouts	896
Career ERA	3.06
Career WHIP	1.13

TRIPLE PLAY:

★ First player named Madison to play in Major League

★ Pitched eight shutout innings to win Game 4 of the 2010 World Series

★ Bumgarner won a career-high 18 games in 2014

Miguel Cabrera

1B/3B/LF/DH	DETROIT TIGERS
THROWS: RIGHT	BATS: RIGHT
HEIGHT: 6' 4"	WEIGHT: 240 LBS	HOMETOWN: MARACAY, VENEZUELA

Sometimes a great start can lead to a great career. In the first Major League game he ever played in 2003, Miguel Cabrera hit a walk-off home run. Then, in that year's World Series, he hit a big homer off super-ace Roger Clemens to help the Marlins win their second championship. But Cabrera was just getting started. In the next four seasons with the Marlins, he topped 112 RBI each year and made four All-Star teams.

In 2007, the Marlins traded their star to Detroit. The American League suited this right-handed batter; he led the AL with 37 homers in his first season with the Tigers. In 2010, he led the league with 126 RBI. Then, showing he was much more than just a home-run hitter, in 2011 he won the first of three straight league batting titles.

In 2012, however, Cabrera really pulled it all together. By leading the AL in homers (44), RBI (139), and average

BASEBALL CARD!

Made the Majors in . . .	2003
Career Avg.	.320
Career OPS	.960
Home Runs	390
RBI	1,369
Runs	1,165

TRIPLE PLAY:

★ Full name is José Miguel Torres Cabrera

★ Has been named to nine All-Stars Games, seven at either first or third base

★ Won Hank Aaron Award as the league's top batter in 2012 and 2013

(.330), he became the first player to win the Triple Crown since 1967! He captured the first of two straight AL MVP awards that year, too.

Cabrera grew up in Venezuela, where the Marlins discovered him and signed him in 1999. Along with being a hitting star, he's a versatile athlete. Cabrera started as an outfielder, but has played well at first and third bases, too. He also serves as the Tigers' designated hitter in many games.

What's next for Cabrera? With such a great start and a solid career so far, he wants to get back to the World Series . . . this time with Detroit.

HISTORY LESSON

When you talk about Tigers' sluggers, you have to include Hank Greenberg. The big Hall of Fame first baseman set a team record with 58 home runs back in 1938.

Yu Darvish

PITCHER	TEXAS RANGERS	
THROWS: RIGHT	BATS: RIGHT	
HEIGHT: 6' 5"	WEIGHT: 215 LBS	HOMETOWN: HABIKINO, JAPAN

It's one thing to be a star in one country . . . it's a big bonus to do it in two! Pitcher Yu Darvish grew up in Japan to become one of the best pitchers that baseball-loving country had ever seen. Then he came to America and has been dazzling hitters ever since.

Yu was one of the top high school pitchers in Japan. He led his team to the national high school championship playoffs twice. Then he jumped right to the Japanese pro league in 2005. By his second year, he had helped them win the Pacific League pennant, their first since 1981, and then helped them win the Japan Series championship for the first time since 1961. In 2007, he won Japan's version of the Cy Young Award, the Samurai, with a 1.82 ERA. He earned two more of the awards in his seven

amazing seasons in Japan, where he was clearly one of the best—if not *the* best— hurlers in the land.

He showed his stuff to the world in the 2009 World Baseball Classic. While striking out 20 batters in 13 innings, he earned two wins and also shut down the US team in a ninth-inning appearance. Darvish clinched it as the closer of the championship game win over South Korea.

After seven seasons in Japan, with a career ERA of 1.99, Yu turned his sights to the Major Leagues. The Texas Rangers paid over $51 million just to get the rights to offer him a contract. He signed with Texas for the 2012 season.

By his second season he was settling in. His 277 strikeouts in 2013 led the Major Leagues and he made his second of three All-Star teams. By 2014, he had lowered his ERA to 3.06, though an arm injury limited him to only 22 starts. At just 28 years old and with great success behind him, he looks to continue his international all-star career!

BASEBALL CARD!

Made the Majors in . . .	2012
Wins*	39
Strikeouts	680
Career ERA	3.27
Career WHIP	1.20

(*Darvish stats for MLB only.)

TRIPLE PLAY:

★ Yu's father is from Iran; Yu's full name is Sefat Farid Yu Darvish

★ In 2011, Yu gave more than $600,000 to help victims of an earthquake in Japan

★ Has been named to the All-Star Game each of his three MLB seasons

Yu Darvish

Jacoby Ellsbury

OUTFIELD | NEW YORK YANKEES

THROWS: LEFT	BATS: LEFT	
HEIGHT: 6' 1"	WEIGHT: 195 LBS	HOMETOWN: MADRAS, OR

In 2007, the Boston Red Sox added a new kind of weapon: speed. That year, rookie center fielder Jacoby Ellsbury burst onto the team late in the year. He stole eight bases in a month, then added a pair in the postseason. In those playoffs, he ended up batting .360, including .438 in the World Series, which Boston won over Colorado.

For the next few seasons, Ellsbury continued to show off his incredible speed. He led the AL with 50 steals in 2008, his first full season in the bigs. He topped that with a Major League best— 70 stolen bases in 2009! He even topped the AL with 10 triples that year.

An injury forced him to miss a lot of time in 2010, but he came back in a big way. In 2011, he showed that he was much more than just a bag-swiper. He hit a career-high 32 homers among his 212 hits and led the AL in total bases. All the while, he patrolled Boston's oddly shaped center field, snagging ball after ball. He was given the Gold Glove in 2011 for his defensive skills. To top off his magic season, he was named the AL Comeback Player of the Year.

Two years later, in 2013, he helped Boston win another World Series, stealing a league-best 52 bases along the way before stealing six more in the postseason!

As good as he was, though, Boston let him become a free agent, so he signed with the Yankees for the 2014 season.

Ellsbury remains one of the top base-stealing threats in the Majors. If he can do for the Yankees what he did for the Red Sox, he might become a hero in another city very soon.

BASEBALL CARD!

Made the Majors in . . .	2007
Career Avg.	.293
Career OPS	.782
Home Runs	81
RBI	384
SBs	280

TRIPLE PLAY:

★ Was also a basketball and football star in high school

★ In 2011, became first Boston player with 30 HRs and 30 SBs in same season

★ First Navajo Native American in Major Leagues; his mother is Navajo

HISTORY LESSON

A stolen base was crucial for the Red Sox in 2004. In the ninth inning of Game 4 of the ALCS, Dave Roberts stole second. He later scored a tying run that kicked off Boston's record-setting comeback. They beat the Yankees in the series after trailing three games to none.

Alex Gordon

OUTFIELD | KANSAS CITY ROYALS

THROWS: RIGHT	BATS: LEFT	
HEIGHT: 6' 1"	WEIGHT: 220 LBS	HOMETOWN: LINCOLN, NE

A lex Gordon is certainly a solid hitter. He had a tie-breaking homer in the 10th inning of Game 1 of the 2014 ALCS, part of his 11 RBI in the postseason. In the World Series, his ninth-inning triple nearly let Kansas City come back and tie Game 7, but he was stranded on-base to end the season. His work with his glove, though, is what has made him an All-Star. In 2014, he flashed the leather in front of a national audience. He made a series of amazing catches in left field as Kansas City nearly won that World Series.

Great fielding is nothing new for Gordon. He has won the outfield Gold Glove award four times in his career. In 2014, he was the AL winner of the Platinum Glove award, given to the top overall fielder in the league, regardless of position. Not bad for a guy who started his big-league career at third base!

Kansas City fans expected big things from Gordon when he arrived in town in 2007. He had had an outstanding minor-league career. That came after he was made the second overall pick of the 2005 amateur draft. Gordon grew up in Nebraska, where he won numerous all-state and All-America honors. He later starred at the University of Nebraska.

In 2011 he had his best season yet, setting career highs in homers and RBI and winning his first Gold Glove. He quickly became the key bat in the young Royals' lineup. Other top players arrived to help him and the result was the team's amazing 2014 run.

Gordon was in the middle of all the Royals' big wins in the playoffs. They won the wild-card playoff game, then beat the Angels and Orioles before stretching the Giants to seven games. It was Kansas City's first postseason since 1985 . . . but if Gordon has anything to say about it, it won't be their last.

HISTORY LESSON

The key player for the Royals in their previous World Series run was third baseman George Brett. The Hall of Famer won three AL batting titles. His .390 average in 1980 was the second highest since Ted Williams hit .406 in 1941.

BASEBALL CARD!

Made the Majors in . . .	2007
Career Avg.	.268
Career OPS	.780
Home Runs	121
RBI	475
Runs	565

TRIPLE PLAY:

★ Won the Dick Howser and Golden Spikes awards as 2005 college player of the year

★ In 2006, Alex was named the minor-league player of the year

★ Father and three brothers all played college baseball

Felix Hernandez

PITCHER	SEATTLE MARINERS	
THROWS: RIGHT	BATS: RIGHT	
HEIGHT: 6' 3"	WEIGHT: 225 LBS	HOMETOWN: VALENCIA, VENEZUELA

Sometimes a great pitcher rises above his team to stand out, even when the team is struggling. That's the case with "King" Felix Hernandez. Since he joined the Seattle rotation in 2006, he has been one of baseball's most feared starters. Big and powerful, he blows hitters away, averaging more than six strikeouts per start. He's also reliable. He has started at least 30 games every season since 2006. But he has had to pitch for a Mariners team that has rarely given him a lot of support. They have won more than half of their games only three times in his career and have never made the playoffs.

That is certainly not Hernandez's fault. He has won at least a dozen games every year except 2008 and has ERAs under 3.50 in the past seven seasons. He led the league with a 2.14 mark in 2014, so he's certainly not slowing down.

In 2010, Hernandez earned his first Cy Young Award (so far!). He won only

BASEBALL CARD!

Made the Majors in . . .	2005
Wins	125
Strikeouts	1,951
Career ERA	3.07
Career WHIP	1.17

TRIPLE PLAY:

★ His fastball was clocked at 94 miles per hour . . . when he was 14!

★ He hit a grand slam off fellow Venezuelan Johan Santana in 2008

★ Named 2014 AL pitcher of the year by *The Sporting News*

13 games that season and even lost 12. But voters who were paying attention knew just how good he was.

Hernandez grew up in Venezuela, a South American country that loves baseball. He was a superstar early and signed a pro contract when he was only 16. His fastball was a legend in the minor leagues in America, as he blew away young hitters game after game. After a great burst in the Majors in 2005, he struggled in his second season. But he learned how to take better care of his body and quickly turned things around. He hasn't looked back since. On a team that is still looking for a way to the playoffs, King Felix is showing them how to win.

HISTORY LESSON

Hernandez is following in the footsteps of other great players from Venezuela. Shortstop Luis Aparicio was the first to make the Baseball Hall of Fame. Dave Concepcion won a pair of World Series with the Reds. Sluggers Magglio Ordóñez and Andrés Galarraga are from there, too.

Felix Hernandez

Clayton Kershaw

PITCHER | LOS ANGELES DODGERS

THROWS: LEFT	BATS: LEFT	
HEIGHT: 6' 4"	WEIGHT: 225 LBS	HOMETOWN: DALLAS, TX

No pitcher in baseball has been as good in the past five years as Clayton Kershaw. If he keeps this up, they might have to change the name of the Cy Young Award. He has put his name on three of them in the past four seasons and there's no sign he won't keep winning them.

In 2014, the Dodgers' ace lefty became the first player ever to lead the Majors in ERA four straight seasons. In fact, he missed the first month of 2014 and still led the Majors with 21 wins and a tiny 0.857 WHIP as well as six complete games. He capped off his marvelous season by earning the NL MVP award. He was the first NL pitcher to grab that hardware since 1968!

In June he threw his first career no-hitter. His 15 strikeouts in that game were the most ever for a no-hitter with no walks. Only an error by a teammate kept him from pitching a perfect game.

A big reason for Kershaw's success, along with a fiery competitive streak, is that he can throw at least three pitches for strikes. His fastball is deadly, but his mighty curveball buckles the knees of the best hitters. Add to that a slider that falls off the table, and it's no wonder he led the Majors in 2004 with an average of 10.8 strikeouts per nine innings.

Kershaw grew up near Dallas. As a high school senior, he struck out 139 batters in only 64 innings! The Dodgers chose him in the first round of the 2006 draft. By 2008, he was the youngest player in the Majors at age 20. In 2011, he took off, starting his ERA-title streak with 21 wins to lead the NL and earn his first Cy Young Award. At only 26 years old and already with Hall of Fame stats, there's no telling how many more Kershaw, er, Cy Young Awards he can earn!

HISTORY LESSON

Kershaw is fast approaching the accomplishments of another Dodgers ace lefty. In the early 1960s, Sandy Koufax threw four no-hitters, led the NL in ERA five straight times, and won three Cy Young Awards. He's atop some experts' lists as the best pitcher of all time.

BASEBALL CARD!

Made the Majors in . . .	2008
Wins	98
Strikeouts	1,445
Career ERA	2.48
Career WHIP	1.06

TRIPLE PLAY:

* In high school, won a game in which he struck out all 15 opposing batters
* Earned baseball's 2012 Roberto Clemente Award for community service
* Kershaw and his wife travel each off-season to Zambia, where they have built an orphanage

Clayton Kershaw

Andrew McCutchen

OUTFIELD | PITTSBURGH PIRATES

THROWS: RIGHT	BATS: RIGHT	
HEIGHT: 5' 10"	WEIGHT: 190 LBS	HOMETOWN: FORT MEADE, FL

The Pittsburgh Pirates are one of the oldest teams in the National League. They have been around since 1887. They played in the first World Series in 1903. They last won a World Series back in 1979. From 1993 to 2012, they didn't even have one winning season. It was a long dry spell for a proud and historic franchise.

But then an exciting young outfielder came into his prime. Andrew McCutchen grew up in Florida, where he was a multi-sport star. Baseball was his best sport, though. As a senior, he hit .700 with 45 stolen bases! The Pirates chose him with their first pick in the 2005 draft.

In 2009, McCutchen became the Pirates' starting center fielder midway through the year . . . and he has never left. In 2013, McCutchen and his all-around excellent game led Pittsburgh back to the postseason.

McCutchen can do it all. He hits clutch homers (in a 2014 game against

BASEBALL CARD!

Made the Majors in . . .	2009
Career Avg.	.299
Career OPS	.883
Home Runs	128
RBI	462
Runs	548
SBs	143

TRIPLE PLAY:

★ In high school, was a Florida state sprinting champion
★ Led the NL in hits in 2012 with 194
★ Has been named to four NL All-Star teams

Cincinnati he tied the game with one homer and then won it two innings later with another), can steal bases (an average of 23 per season in six seasons), get on base (he led the Majors with a .410 on-base percentage in 2014), and he can play great defense (he won a Gold Glove in 2012). Put it all together and you've got a special player.

The peak of his career so far was that 2013 season. That was the season that the Pirates finally broke their jinx, winning 94 games and earning their first playoff game since 1992. He was disappointed when the Pirates lost in the NL Division Series. But he enjoyed big news in the off-season. McCutchen got 28 out of 30 votes to win the NL MVP award.

HISTORY LESSON

Another great Pirates outfielder who also threw and hit right-handed was Roberto Clemente. The rocket-armed right fielder won four NL batting titles and a record-tying 12 Gold Gloves, and helped the Pirates win two World Series. After he was killed in 1972 in a plane crash on the way to help earthquake victims in Nicaragua, he was elected to the Hall of Fame.

Andrew McCutchen

Yadier Molina

CATCHER | ST. LOUIS CARDINALS

THROWS: RIGHT	BATS: RIGHT	
HEIGHT: 5' 11"	WEIGHT: 220 LBS	HOMETOWN: BAYAMON, PUERTO RICO

In the past decade, the best catcher has been Yadier Molina. He has certainly been solid with the bat, with four .300-plus seasons and three top-10 rankings in batting average. But it's Yadi's work behind the plate that makes him a star. He has won the last seven Gold Gloves for his position in the NL. He has also won three of the four Platinum Gloves for the NL since the award debuted in 2011; those go to the single player voted best defender in each league, regardless of position. Plus, with his rocket arm, Yadi throws out a higher percentage of opponents trying to steal than almost any other catcher every year. And on a team with a solid corps of veterans, he is the certain leader.

Molina grew up in Puerto Rico and was drafted by the Cardinals in 2000. He was following his brothers into the catcher's box. Bengie joined the Angels in 1998, while Jose joined the Cubs in 1999. For seven years—from 2004 to

BASEBALL CARD!

Made the Majors in . . .	2004
Career Avg.	.284
Career OPS	.741
Home Runs	96
RBI	584
Runs	451

TRIPLE PLAY:

⭐ Yadier's brothers, Bengie and Jose were both big-league catchers

⭐ The Molina brothers' father, Benjamin, is in the Puerto Rico Baseball Hall of Fame

⭐ Yadier has been named to six NL All-Star teams

2010—there were three Molinas handling big-league pitching! But Yadier has emerged as the best of the family. He reached the Majors in 2004 and helped the Cardinals reach the World Series that year. Then he was behind the plate when they won it all in 2006.

In 2008, his average got above .300 for the first time and he started his Gold Glove streak. Often, a catcher has to grow into his leadership role. As Molina got older, that's just what he did. In 2011, he was a key part of the Cardinals' NL-record eleventh World Series championship. They returned to the Fall Classic in 2013 but lost to Boston.

HISTORY LESSON

More than 350 sets of brothers have played in the Major Leagues. A trio similar to the Molinas was the DiMaggios, who played in the 1940s. Joe D. was a Hall of Fame outfielder and one of the greatest Yankees ever. Vince played for several teams, while Dom was a great outfielder for the Red Sox for a decade.

Yadier Molina

David Ortiz

DH | BOSTON RED SOX

THROWS: LEFT	BATS: LEFT	
HEIGHT: 6' 3"	WEIGHT: 230 LBS	HOMETOWN: SANTO DOMINGO, DOMINICAN REPUBLIC

It's hard to say which is bigger: David Ortiz's powerful bat, his leadership on the three-time champion Red Sox, or his amazing smile! The man they call "Big Papi" might say that the biggest thing about him is his heart.

In 2004, Ortiz set a career high, to that point, with 139 RBI. He also had 41 homers and the Red Sox made the playoffs. In the ALCS, they made history. Trailing the Yankees three games to none, they came back to win four straight. Big Papi won the first of those games with a 12th-inning homer. He did it again in the next game, singling in the winning run in the 14th inning. And he added a two-run shot in Game 7 as the Sox clinched it (Ortiz was the ALCS MVP, of course). In the World Series, he

had a homer and four RBI, and the Red Sox won their first title since 1918!

But he and the Red Sox were not done yet. Big Papi had monster years in 2005 and 2006, and Boston returned to the World Series in 2007. He had four RBI as the Sox swept the Rockies for another title.

By then, Big Papi was one of baseball's biggest stars, thanks to his big bat, clutch hitting, and super-fun personality. He always seemed to be ready with a laugh or with a game-winning homer.

In 2013, the Red Sox put together an amazing season, they won their third World Series title since 2004. Big Papi was at the center of it all, of course. He hit .309 that season with 103 RBI. But in the World Series, he was even better. He slugged two homers and set a record with a .688 average. The Sox beat the Cardinals and he was named World Series MVP!

As a slugger or as a leader, Big Papi is definitely one thing: a winner.

HISTORY LESSON

The designated hitter rule was added to baseball in 1973. It was a way to get more offense into a game that was dominated by pitchers in those days. Ron Blomberg of the Yankees got the first at-bat by a DH. He walked! Today, the NL is the only pro league in the world that does not use the DH.

BASEBALL CARD!

Made the Majors in . . .	1997
Career Avg.	.285
Career OPS	.926
Home Runs	466
RBI	1,533
Runs	1,267

TRIPLE PLAY:

★ David's father, Leo, played baseball in their native Dominican Republic

★ Led the Majors with 148 RBI in 2005 and led AL with 54 homers in 2006

★ Has the most hits of any DH in history

Buster Posey

CATCHER | SAN FRANCISCO GIANTS

THROWS: RIGHT	BATS:RIGHT	
HEIGHT: 6' 1"	WEIGHT: 215 LBS	HOMETOWN: LEESBURG, GA

Buster Posey must think this stuff is easy. He has played four full seasons with the Giants . . . and they have won the World Series in three of those years! Then again, maybe it's the Giants who should be thinking, "Thank goodness we've got Buster on our side!"

Posey has become one of the best-hitting catchers ever. His .336 average in 2012 led the league; he was the first NL catcher to do that since 1942!

Posey grew up in Georgia in a sports-crazy family. His brothers played basketball and his sister was a softball star. Buster became one of the top stars in the state while also playing several positions in the field. He moved on to Florida State as a pitcher and by 2008, he was one of the best all-around college

players in the nation. In one 10–0 victory over Savannah State he played all nine positions and hit a grand slam! The Giants chose him fifth overall in 2008 and paid him a record signing bonus of $6.2 million.

That's a lot of pressure to put on a young player, but Buster had no problems. He was called up to the Giants at the end of 2009; then, in 2010, he helped them reach the playoffs and the World Series. Plus, he was the NL Rookie of the Year. No rookie catcher had played for a World Series team and batted cleanup since 1947! But he hit .300 and the Giants won their first Series title since 1954!

Posey won the 2012 batting title, was named the NL MVP, and led San Francisco to yet another Series win. They repeated the feat in 2014, as Buster caught the amazing Madison Bumgarner's record pitching streak.

HISTORY LESSON

Buster and the Giants won the Series in 2010, 56 years after the team last won the Fall Classic. In that win, they were led by Hall of Famer Willie Mays. He was one of the greatest all-around players ever, able to hit, run, and field like few others. The "Say Hey Kid," as he was known, hit 660 career homers!

BASEBALL CARD!

Made the Majors in . . .	2009
Career Avg.	.308
Career OPS	.861
Home Runs	83
RBI	352
Runs	287

TRIPLE PLAY:

★ Buster's real first name is Gerald

★ As a high school junior, he pitched his team to a state title, hitting a grand slam to clinch it

★ Has won two Silver Slugger Awards as top hitter at his position

24

Giancarlo Stanton

OUTFIELD | MIAMI MARLINS

THROWS: RIGHT	BATS: RIGHT

HEIGHT: 6' 6"	WEIGHT: 240 LBS	HOMETOWN: PANORAMA CITY, CA

Baseball is all about the numbers. In 2014, Giancarlo Stanton put his name on one of the biggest numbers yet. The power-hitting young outfielder signed a contract with the Miami Marlins that will pay him up to $325 million through 2027.

If any young player is worth that much, it just might be Giancarlo, who was known as Mike Stanton in his early playing days. He switched to his actual first name in 2012.

Giancarlo grew up in the San Fernando Valley, just north of Los Angeles. He was an awesome athlete in high school—he was all-conference in both hoops and football. But he played a lot of baseball on travel teams, and got better and better. After a scout saw him in an all-star game, he was chosen by the Marlins in the 2007 draft.

Before he had turned 20, he hit nearly 100 homers in the minors. The Marlins couldn't wait any longer and called him up to the big club in 2010. In his first game, he had three hits and scored a pair of runs! He soon showed the home-run

BASEBALL CARD!

Made the Majors in . . .	2010
Career Avg.	.271
Career OPS	.903
Home Runs	154
RBI	399
Runs	350

TRIPLE PLAY:

★ Known as Gene or Carlos when he was a kid before settling on Mike in fifth grade and then changing it again in the Majors

★ First big-league home run was a grand slam against the Tampa Bay Rays

★ Got a scare in late 2014 when hit in the face by a pitch but is recovering well

power that had dominated the minors. In only 101 games as a rookie, he hit 22 dingers, then had 34 more in 2011, fifth in the NL. He shocked onlookers during a batting practice session at Dodger Stadium by hitting a ball completely out of the park. That has only happened twice during an actual game in the park's 52-year history.

It was the 2014 season that really cemented Giancarlo's place as baseball's best right-handed slugger. He led the NL with 37 homers and had a career-high 105 RBI. He finished second in the race for NL MVP behind pitcher Clayton Kershaw.

HISTORY LESSON

The Marlins joined the NL as an expansion team in 1993. In 1997, they won the World Series. At the time, that was the fastest championship ever by a new team.

Giancarlo Stanton

Mike Trout

OUTFIELD | LOS ANGELES ANGELS

THROWS: RIGHT	BATS: RIGHT

HEIGHT: 6' 2"	WEIGHT: 230 LBS	HOMETOWN: VINELAND, NJ

Is Mike Trout the best player in baseball? Most experts—and millions of fans—would say, "Yes!" In his first three full seasons, he finished second twice in the AL MVP race and then won the award outright in 2014. He has led the league in runs three times. He was the 2012 AL Rookie of the Year, a three-time All-Star, and a three-time Silver Slugger winner. And at the start of the 2015 season . . . he'll be only 23 years old!

Mike grew up in New Jersey, where he was a star from a young age. In high school, he was one of the top players in the nation. The Angels snagged him in the first round of the 2009 draft.

In the late spring of 2012, the Angels were struggling. They needed a spark. Mike proved to be what they needed. In June he had more runs than anyone in baseball. He was leading the AL in steals and batting at the All-Star break.

Mike was showing that he was a great hitter for sure, clubbing homers and driving balls into the gaps. But it was his blinding speed that set him apart. A simple ground ball to short became an adventure for the defense as Mike churned the dirt toward first. But as great as he is, fans really love him for his humble attitude. He still lives near his parents in the off-season and always talks about his team first.

Mike was the youngest player ever to win MVP on a unanimous vote after leading the AL with 111 RBI and 115 runs. One of baseball's newest hot stats is WAR: Wins Above Replacement. That means a player is worth X number of wins more than an average player. Trout has had the best WAR in the AL for three straight years, including a high of 10.8 in his rookie season.

If you're in a baseball battle, you want to go to WAR with Mike Trout!

HISTORY LESSON

Mike's combination of power and speed calls to mind another great young player, Yankees outfielder Mickey Mantle. He won three MVP awards in the 1950s and '60s and ended up with 536 homers in his Hall of Fame career.

BASEBALL CARD!

Made the Majors in . . .	2011
Career Avg.	.305
Career OPS	.945
Home Runs	98
RBI	307
Runs	373

TRIPLE PLAY:

★ Mike's dad, Jeff, played minor league baseball in the Twins' organization

★ In a high school playoff game, Mike was once walked intentionally with the bases loaded!

★ Mike was the 2014 MLB All-Star Game MVP

Throwing Heat!

Baseball today boasts a ton of top strikeout pitchers. Batters are whiffing at record rates. A big reason for that is a crop of outstanding fireballers mowing them down! Here's a look at some of the hardest-throwing pitchers in the game:

Stephen Strasburg

WASHINGTON NATIONALS

Busting pitches at more than 100 miles per hour, Stephen exploded onto the baseball scene in 2010. But an arm injury slowed his rise to the top. After surgery, he came back firing. In 2014, he had his best year yet, tying for the NL lead with 242 Ks, an average of more than 10 for every nine innings.

Corey Kluber

CLEVELAND INDIANS

After two pretty good seasons, Kluber shot to the top of the charts in 2014. He was second in the AL with 269 strikeouts and led the league with 18 wins. A big right-hander with a blazing fastball, he was named the AL Cy Young Award winner.

Johnny Cueto
CINCINNATI REDS

Johnny's twisting delivery makes it hard to see some of his pitches. Of course, some of them are going so fast, it doesn't matter! In a league packed with power pitchers, his 242 Ks were tied for tops in 2014. Add to that a 2.25 ERA and you've got an all-around ace.

Craig Kimbrel
ATLANTA BRAVES

A closer wants to come in and shut the other team down. He wants to stop a rally or prevent it from starting. The best way? Just don't let them hit the ball. San Diego's newest closer has done just that, leading the NL in saves the past two seasons and tying for the lead the two seasons before that. Along the way, he has mowed down hitters at a record pace. Among pitchers with at least 250 career innings, Craig's average of 14.2 strikeouts per nine innings is second all-time!

2014 MLB
Final Standings

AMERICAN LEAGUE

AL EAST

BALTIMORE ORIOLES	96–66
NEW YORK YANKEES	84–78
TORONTO BLUE JAYS	83–79
TAMPA BAY RAYS	77–85
BOSTON RED SOX	71–91

AL CENTRAL

DETROIT TIGERS	90–72
KANSAS CITY ROYALS	89–73
CLEVELAND INDIANS	85–77
CHICAGO WHITE SOX	73–89
MINNESOTA TWINS	70–92

AL WEST

LOS ANGELES ANGELS	98–64
OAKLAND ATHLETICS	88–74
SEATTLE MARINERS	87–75
HOUSTON ASTROS	70–92
TEXAS RANGERS	67–95

NATIONAL LEAGUE

NL EAST

WASHINGTON NATIONALS	96–66
ATLANTA BRAVES	79–83
NEW YORK METS	79–83
MIAMI MARLINS	77–85
PHILADELPHIA PHILLIES	73–89

NL CENTRAL

ST. LOUIS CARDINALS	90–72
PITTSBURGH PIRATES	88–74
MILWAUKEE BREWERS	82–80
CINCINNATI REDS	76–86
CHICAGO CUBS	73–89

NL WEST

LOS ANGELES DODGERS	94–68
SAN FRANCISCO GIANTS	88–74
SAN DIEGO PADRES	77–85
COLORADO ROCKIES	66–96
ARIZONA DIAMONDBACKS	64–98